Great Leaders Never Climb Smooth Mountains

*How To Avoid The 17½ Routes
To Ineffective Leadership*

John Keith Edington

THE OLD SCHOOL
CONSTABLE BURTON
LEYBURN, NORTH YORKSHIRE
DL85RG

© 2013 JOHN EDINGTON. ALL RIGHTS RESERVED

ALL RIGHTS RESERVED. NO PART OF THIS WORK MAY BE REPRODUCED OR STORED IN AN INFORMATIONAL RETRIEVAL SYSTEM, WITHOUT THE EXPRESS PERMISSION OF THE PUBLISHER IN WRITING

BOOK COVER DESIGNED BY:
SARA ROBISH
WWW.SARAROBISHART.COM
"Fantastic work once again Sara, thank you"

BOOK LAYOUT & FORMATTING BY: ACCESS IDEAS
EMAIL: ACCESS.IDEAS@YAHOO.COM
"Great work guys, see you on my next book"

ISBN 978-1-291-41345-8

AUTHOR OF:
- People Know What To Do So Why the HELL Don't They Do it?
- Everything I learnt About Leadership I Learnt From A Pineapple; 9½ Refreshing Leadership Facts
- You Cannot Lead The Cavalry Charge If You Think You Look Silly On A Horse"
- Developing A Leadership Mindset

PERSONAL INVITATION TO INCREASE YOUR BOTTOM LINE PROFIT AT NO EXTRA PRODUCTION COSTS

I am John Edington; I am currently working with several companies to assist them to be the best they can be.

What exactly does that mean I hear you say?

There are five major areas that you will benefit from when partaking in The Psychology Leadership Mastery Programme:

1. Become the person company's fight to keep. You have invested a lot of time, effort and money into your career this far; in this uncertain economic time, The Psychology Leadership Mastery programme will help you get the best return on your investment in you.

2. Establishing a rewarding career does not always mean a higher salary it can also mean you acquire the prestige, status and influence that will carry you through all areas of your life.

3. Become the person people look up no matter how tall they grow! Learn how to form and maintain lasting relationships in work and in your personal life that are built on Trust and Respect.

4. Become the best you can be. Be the master of your own destiny. Experience the challenge of opening up whole new areas of your life and feel the excitement of practicing new skills that will help you get the best out of life.

5. All human beings have an in built desire to be emotionally connected with life. We need to feel alive, have meaning and purpose in our lives. We do not have time for boredom and mindless repetition.

The mindset system taught in the leadership programme has been tried tested and proven by 1233 of the world's most successful business leaders.

If you have any questions regarding my invitation please call me on 01224 548 814

I promise you no hard sell no pressure just two professionals discussing how to increase bottom line profit at no extra production costs.

Warm regards

John

ACKNOWLEDGEMENTS

I would like to thank my clients for all their feedback and responses that have contributed to the content of this book.

To the private and corporate clients, who have attended my workshops and seminars and shared their valuable knowledge for us all to learn from.

To Moira, my wife, for her love and support thank you.

Simon Gilbert, for all your help, guidance and above all, your knowledge; a true friend and mentor, thank you.

Alison Watt and Anna Corbett for your honest feedback;

Thank you for transforming your knowledge into positive action

Kevin Downie for all his advice and creative talent in web design kevin@websites-etc.co.uk

Richard Boyd from Redflame Marketing, first class marketing advice, a true gentleman

And finally, my fellow mastermind group members, where our several minds will always prove that the whole is greater than the sum of the parts.

Vision without action is a daydream
Action without vision is a nightmare

Japanese Proverb

CONTENTS

Why Is It That Nobody Goes To The Guru At The Bottom Of The Mountain?	1
Why The Psychology Of Leadership Mastery Makes The Difference	3
If You Only Sold Envelopes	7
Why Me, Why This, Why Now?	13
The Psychology Of Leadership Mastery	15
4 Steps To The Top Of The Mountain	19
17½ Proven Ways	23
Rule One Understand The Importance Of Building Self Esteem And Confidence	27
Rule Two Confidence Respect Efficacy Worthiness	29
Rule Three Past And Current Events Impact On The Psychology Of Leadership Mastery Results.	33
Rule Four Deal With The Fear Of Change	37
Rule Five Learning Needs Time To Fully Integrate Into New Behaviour And Actions	39
Rule Six Off The Shelf Programmes Are Considerably Less Effective.	45
Rule Seven Involve, Inspire And Ignite	47

Rule Eight   49
Employee Engagement Is Vital

Rule Nine   51
*Improvements Are Adequately
Measured Before And After Training*

Rule Ten   53
*Training Must Be Provided With
Corresponding Changes In Performance
Expectations Or Performance Reviews*

Rule Eleven   55
*Tell Your Employees Your Desired
Outcome; Always Remain Clear
And Specific About Your Expectations*

Rule Twelve   59
*Only Use A Trainer That Is Enthusiastic,
Credible, Experienced And Comfortable
In Even The Most Challenging Group
Environments.*

Rule Thirteen   63
*87% Of Employees Have Switched Off
Within Six Months Of Joining A Company.*

Rule Fourteen   65
*Extensive Research Has Shown That
Trainers With The Correct Qualifications
Yield A Higher Return On Investment.*

Rule Fifteen   69
The Art Of Influencing Other

Rule Sixteen   71
The Frank Sinatra Principle

Rule Seventeen   73
The Four Laws Of Successful

Rule Seventeen And A Half   75
Worthwhile Work

Summary Of The Rules   87

WHY IS IT THAT NOBODY GOES TO THE GURU AT THE BOTTOM OF THE MOUNTAIN

K2 is the world's second largest mountain; K2 is also called Ketu in the local Balti language. Why is this so important? According to Mayan, Egyptian and Vedic traditions Ketu represents the **Transformation of Knowledge into Positive Action**

The Psychology of Leadership Mastery is founded on the principles of transforming knowledge into positive action.

The summit of K2/Ketu is said to be the place where the legendary Hall of Records are hidden. These records contain all of man's and woman's accomplishments. It would naturally follow that in order to access the wisdom contained in the Hall of Records, you must firstly choose to begin the journey to the summit. Leaders know that there will be setback on the journey to the summit. Avoiding as many obstacles and setbacks as possible makes the journey easier as prevention is always better than cure.

The second part of the journey is the transformation of the new found knowledge in 2 positive action using

THE PSYCHOLOGY OF LEADERSHIP MASTERY

This is no ordinary book you are holding in your hands. Join the author on this metaphorical ancient quest, a dramatic journey in the footsteps of Alexander the Great who was considered one of the most successful leaders of all time.

To the highest peaks of your professional development; and the very heart of the Himalayas Hall of Records... a journey of transformation of knowledge into positive action that is wholly focused in converting knowledge into action.

Designed from the results of leading psychological research and the 24 years practical application of turning leadership knowledge into positive actions that

Inspires Both Your Employees and Customers To Be Involved In Igniting Your Bottom Line Profit

WHY THE PSYCHOLOGY OF LEADERSHIP MASTERY MAKES THE DIFFERENCE

I started to study the psychology of achievement some 24 years ago as a result of owning and running several successful businesses.

My problem was not being a success, it was that I was working 18 hours a day seven days a week and both my mind and body decided to let me know that all was not well.

I first started to study stress seeing as my body was not too happy with my current way of working.

I then went on to study why other successful business owners appeared to be happier and achieve more with their lives, career and businesses than I was.

My whole life totally changed after I had attended my first psychology of achievement course. My inner light bulb finely came on and I just knew I had found my true vocation.

I will always remember my wife asking me if I was feeling OK as I gazed out of the lounge window.

Yes and no I replied, yes I said because my whole life has just changed as a result of the psychology course I had attended. I tried to explain why I had said no, "it's as if everything that I thought was important in my life was no longer important and that I could still be successful in any area of my life without the need to work 18 hours a day 356 days a year. I just didn't know how to do it right now"

My journey had begun on the road to finding the answers to "I know what to do so why the hell don't I do it?" and "its knowing how to be different that makes the difference"

I wanted to achieve two things in my life the first was to help me get more from my life and the second is help real people with real problems achieve more while living in the real world.

That was 24 years ago, during that journey I have collected as many of the practical methods that have been tried, tested and proven too achieve more in your life, your career or your business.

The Psychology of Leadership Mastery has evolved as a result of studying three main areas:

1. **Psychology:**

    Psychology is defined as the study of mind and behaviour, the perfect combination for any aspiring leader or business owner to understand and fully integrate into their daily lives.

2. **Leadership:**

    Leadership is defined as the transferring of ideas to the minds of others. How well we transfer those ideas will determine the success we achieve in life, career and business.

3. **Mastery:**

    Mastery is defined as being better today than you were yesterday. Mastery in any subject is a journey not a destination, this way we can continue to improve, achieve and master any area of our lives we choose.

When you put all three together you have the most comprehensive leadership mentoring programme offered anywhere in the UK.

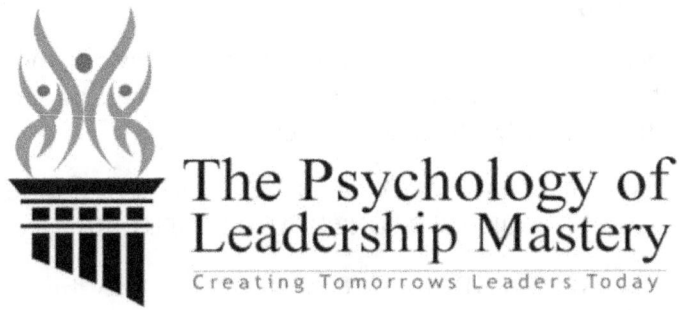

Please contact:
JOHN EDINGTON

www.leadershipmastery.co.uk
Email: john@leadershipmastery.co.uk
Telephone. 01224 548 814

REFLECTION PAGE

SPEND A MOMENT TO REFLECT AND
ASK YOURSELF THE FOLLOWING QUESTIONS

1. Psychology:

Psychology is defined as the study of mind and behaviour, the perfect combination for any aspiring leader or business owner to understand and fully integrate into their daily lives.

- WHAT BEHAVIOUR WOULD YOU LIKE TO CHANGE IN EITHER YOURSELF OR ONE OF YOUR EMPLOYEES?
- WHAT WOULD BE THE BENEFIT OF CHANGING THIS BEHAVIOUR?

2. Leadership:

Leadership is defined as the transferring of ideas to the minds of others. How well we transfer those ideas will determine the success we achieve in life, career and business.

- IF YOU COULD IMPROVE ONE AREA OF COMMUNICATION WHAT WOULD IT BE?

3. Mastery:

Mastery is defined as being better today than you were yesterday. Mastery in any subject is a journey not a destination, this way we can continue to improve, achieve and master any area of our lives we choose.

- WHERE ARE THE CRITICAL AREAS YOU OR YOUR KEY EMPLOYEES NEED TO MASTER?

IF YOU ONLY SOLD ENVELOPES

*"We are what we repeatedly do.
Excellence, then, is not an act, but a habit."*
~ Aristotle ~

What makes this book different from all the other information products and books telling us of the authors' accounts of the accomplishments they have achieved as a business leader / entrepreneur or their vision, creativity and ability to energize, inspire and motivate others towards achieving greatness?

This book is an introduction to a whole new concept in The Psychology of Leadership Mastery for both individuals and employees; the guaranteed **Transformation of Knowledge in 2 Positive Action that Creates Excellence Within People**

The Psychology of Leadership Mastery Programme has been tried, tested and proven on Olympic athletes, the World's and UK's leading employers and some of the countries leading professionals in their field.

According to research by Professor Leonard Sayles, author of *"The Triumph of High Performance over Conventional Management Principles"* states that most information is actually classed as non-information.

What is non-information?

Recently I attended a seminar; I left the seminar with these pearls of non-information:

- To be an effective leader you have to be empathetic.
- Effective leaders must have an ability to motivate others

This sounds on the surface to be excellent advice. The problem with this type of advice is it contains no useful practical information of how to achieve the advice given.

~ Professor Sayles states, ~
"A great many consultants and seminars deliver this type of non-information."

To avoid the non-information style of training, individuals need help in making positive changes

> "It is knowing how to be different that makes the difference"

> "Each moment you have an opportunity to make a difference. Each day you can be the fulfilment that you seek to experience."
> ~ Ralph Marston ~

The Psychology of Leadership Mastery is designed to assist businesses with their greatest asset 'people'.

Leaders are continually mentoring and developing their personnel and those they lead in order to create excellence within people.

YOUR BUSINESS IS NOT ONLY THE PRODUCTS YOU SELL. YOUR BUSINESS IS MORE IMPORTANTLY THE PEOPLE WHO SELL YOUR PRODUCTS.

If every business only sold envelopes why would customers buy from you?

The answer would always be the people who serve them. Your business is both products and people. Creating excellence within people is just as important as creating excellence in your products.

> *"Our most productive investment remains our people. It is through the dedication, skills and initiative of our people that this business has prospered and will continue to move ahead."*
> ~ Richard Pratt ~

In recent years the move from human beings into human capita has failed.

Psychology is defined as the study of mind and behaviour. I apply my 24 year study of mind and behaviour specifically to leadership mastery. Doesn't it make perfect sense if you want to be wealthy you would study wealth, and if you wanted to be happy you would study happiness? The psychology of leadership mastery does what it says on the tin: leadership mastery.

THE PEOPLE WHO SELL YOUR PRODUCTS

Selfridge's department stores highlight a great point with a mirror they have in the staff room. Their full length mirror has written on it

> "This is the customer's
> First impression of you"

What make this even more impressive is the fact that their turnover last year was £655 million. Their bottom line profit was £84 million.

Selfridges pride themselves on selling quality goods. In order to do that the staff must represent the same standard of quality and service.

> "It's not who you are that holds you back,
> it's who you think you're not."
> ~ Author Unknown ~

Imagine inviting the World's leading business experts, and leaders of the top companies in the UK and worldwide into your business to give you practical ways of getting the best out of your most valuable asset, your employees.

What a fantastic experience that would be, having all those years of experience and all that talent working for you.

I would invite you to look upon this book in a similar way to inviting these leading experts of industry and those at the top of their field in the Psychology of Achievement.

Using all their knowledge and expertise coupled with my 24 years' practical experience in the psychology of achievement I have created this practical and proven way of transforming knowledge into positive actions. Positive actions that increase bottom line profit at no extra production costs.

> "It Is Knowing How To Be Different That Makes The Difference " Once a person knows how to be different they create excellence within themselves.

This book highlights the 17 and a half most commonly repeated mistakes that companies make that alienate their entire workforce faster than falling down a mountain.

The Psychology of Leadership Mastery Programme will give you the practical skills you need to guarantee that transformation of your bottom line profit.

"We are what we repeatedly do. Excellence, then, is not an act, but a habit."
~ Aristotle ~

"If you are going to achieve excellence in big things, you develop the habit in little matters. Excellence is not an exception, it is a prevailing attitude."
~ Colin Powell ~

REFLECTION PAGE

TAKE A MINUTE TO REFLECT ON YOUR OBSERVATIONS REGARDING THE MOST COMMONLY REPEATED MISTAKES IN YOUR BUSINESS/ DEPARTMENT, MAKE A LIST

- ---
- ---
- ---
- ---
- ---
- ---
- ---
- ---
- ---
- ---

HAVING MADE YOUR LIST NOW PRIORITISE THEN, WHICH WILL GIVE YOU THE MOST REWARD WHEN CORRECTED?

WHY ME, WHY THIS, WHY NOW?

There is one question that business owners and business leaders frequently ask themselves in relation to their employees.

"People know what to do so why the HELL don't they do it"?

There are times in everybody's life when we will have asked the above question;

Usually at this time we cannot clearly see a way forward. I would like to share with you two reasons why it is so difficult to see the solution to our problems,

> The first from Nobel Prize winner
> ~ Albert Einstein ~
> *"WE CAN'T SOLVE PROBLEMS BY USING THE SAME KIND OF THINKING WE USED WHEN WE CREATED THEM."*
>
> The second reason is based on the research of Psychologist
> ~ Dr J Brothers: ~
> *"WE CANNOT CONSISTENTLY OUT PERFORM THE IMAGE WE HAVE OF OURSELVES"*

This book explores the Why to and How to change both your thinking and the image you have of yourself; therefore creating excellence within your business.

REFLECTION PAGE

SPEND A MOMENT TO REFLECT AND
ASK YOURSELF THE FOLLOWING QUESTIONS

WHICH AREA OF YOUR BUSINESS HAVE YOU RECENTLY ASKED THE FOLLOWING QUESTIONS?

- "People know what to do so why the HELL don't they do it"?

- WHY ME

- WHY THIS

- WHY NOW?

ON REFLECTION WHAT ACTION COULD YOU HAVE IMPLEMENTED TO PREVENT OR REDUCE THE IMPACT OF THE EVENTS?

- ---
- ---
- ---
- ---

THE PSYCHOLOGY OF LEADERSHIP MASTERY

Is designed to assist businesses with their greatest asset 'people'
Leaders are continually mentoring and developing their personnel and those they lead in order to create excellence within people

> The most important question to ask on the job is not "what am I getting? The most important question is "what am I becoming"

This book contains a collection of key ideas that have been found to be so powerful in their personal and professional development.

The ten key points listed below are the building blocks for creating excellence within people.

> Its knowing how to be different that makes the difference

The book shows how you can develop the key traits listed below within yourself and your business.

Imagine the positive difference to your bottom line profit if every employee was giving 100% in the following key traits

Self reliance: *the capacity to manage one's self, make one's own judgments rather than constantly asking others for their judgment.*

Self confidence: *a person's belief that he or she can succeed. Self-confidence has long been thought of as an important determinant of performance. It tends to be self-generating.*

Relationship skills: *a relationship between people should be a state of connectedness involving mutual dealings between people or parties. It is proven psychology that people buy more from people they like.*

Empathy: *A desirable trust-building characteristic. Psychologists inform us that people work harder for employer's they trust. Customers buy more from people they trust.*

Assertiveness: *it's true that angry people need to learn to become assertive (rather than aggressive), but most books and courses on developing assertiveness are aimed at people who don't feel enough anger. That isn't helping the people who struggle with their anger. This can have a major affect on customer relationships.*

Optimism: *a tendency to expect the best possible outcome from themselves and others. Optimistic people will focus on the solution to a problem not just the problem.*

Passion and Enthusiasm: *according to Ralph Waldo Emerson "Nothing great was ever achieved without enthusiasm." Imagine your employees and customers being*

greeted by a person with a passion and enthusiasm for their work.

Self Respect: *without self-respect there can be no genuine success. Success won at the cost of self-respect is not success. People with high self respect are proven to work 30% more productively*

Worthiness: *is said to be the quality or state of having merit or value for the work they do and to the people around them.*

Self Efficacy: *Self-efficacy has been described as the belief that one is capable of performing in a certain manner to attain certain goals. Self-efficacy explicitly refers to your ability to deal with challenging encounters*

Your business will benefit from

THE PSYCHOLOGY OF LEADERSHIP MASTERY

REFLECTION PAGE

WHAT WOULD YOU SCORE YOURSELF OUT OF 10 ON THE FOLLOWING POINTS? 10 BEING EXCELLENT

Self- reliance: ----------------

Self- confidence: ----------------

Relationship skills: ----------------

Empathy: ----------------

Assertiveness: ----------------

Optimism: ----------------

Passion and Enthusiasm: ----------------

Self-Respect: ----------------

Worthiness: ----------------

Self Efficacy: ----------------

4 STEPS TO THE TOP OF THE MOUNTAIN

THE PSYCHOLOGY OF LEADERSHIP MASTERY Delivers a four step process to ensure the lasting success of creating excellence within people

Your 4 simple steps to the top of the mountain

STEP 1: Know What You Want.

George Harrison wrote a song titled "If you don't know where you're going any road will take you there."

Establishing where you want to go is the first step. It is easier to hit the target when you can see it.

If you want to be wealthy would make perfect sense that you would study wealth therefore wouldn't it make equal sense if you wanted to be happy, you would study happiness.

A good objective of leadership is to help those who are doing poorly to do well and to help those who are doing well to do even better, by applying the study of mind and behaviour to your desired outcome give you the maximum opportunity to achieve it. Start by asking what is your desired outcome and the benefits of achieving it?

STEP 2:
Turn Knowledge in 2 Action.

We have all at some time in our lives tried to be healthier, fitter or eat less only to find within a few days we have reverted back to our old comfortable habits. Employees and business leaders are exactly the same; repetition and guidance is the key to **"it is knowing how to be different that makes the difference"**

STEP 3:
Notice What's Working and Not Working.

The programme gives you the benefit of impartial and objective monitoring of what is working and what is not. You may have heard the old saying "You cannot see the wood for the trees".

STEP 4:
Change Your Approach and Try Again.

There is no failure only feedback. Monitoring and adjusting your course up the mountain is essential. Building base camps along the journey ensure that your business can adjust quickly and correctly to the changing landscape.

It's that simple. Now you may want to argue that it's not that easy, but easy or not... it is that simple.

How To Read This Book

You can either read front to back collecting each of the proven ways to seriously **increase** the effectiveness and profitability of your investments in people.

Or you can read an individual chapter and apply it to your current training and mentoring needs.

The book is written a little tongue in cheek but do not let that undermine the research and experience that has gone into the proven ways to seriously reduce the effectiveness and profitability of your investment in people.

This books pulls together the latest tried, tested and proven techniques that some of the World's leading researchers have documented.

It is also the result of over 24 years of practical experience working with business leaders, Olympic athletes and private individuals to creates excellence within people

The inclusion of quotes throughout this book is intentional, they are there to help you reflex on the messages given in each chapter.

There are generally two kinds of books concerning leadership and management; the first is where the individual's leadership skill will be an inspiration to others to follow.

The second is as a warning not to follow this individual. It is usually highlighting where they failed. This book will show you both options.

Each chapter of this book is designed to give you both warning and inspiration.

Follow the most common mistakes as highlighted in the first half of each chapter and you are guaranteed to waste your valuable time and money,

Or you could…

Follow the inspirational aspects in the second half of each chapter where you will guarantee to

Inspire Your Employees and Customers To Be Involved In Igniting Your Bottom Line Profit

> *"An investment in knowledge*
> *Always pays the best interest."*
> ~ Benjamin Franklin ~

GREAT LEADERS NEVER CLIMB SMOOTH MOUNTAINS

You know what it's like; we have all attended training sessions that have no positive impact on our day to day management activities. In fact they have taken away our valuable time and given us back very little in return.

Not only have you paid for the training you have also paid your employees to be away from work for the day. Having paid in time and money you also have a de-motivated and stressed manager.

For 24 years I've been involved with the psychology of achievement in relation to the leadership and management programmes for every level of Manager and employee. I have in that time extensively researched and compiled a tried tested and proven list of how to avoid the 17½ routes to ineffective leadership

> *"Every mountain top is within reach if you just keep climbing."*
> Barry Finlay, Kilimanjaro and Beyond ~

Each of the following proven ways will seriously reduce the effectiveness and profitability of both your investments in people and the profitability of your entire workforce.

In order to transform **Knowledge into Action** you need to succeed in two major areas. The first is motivating the managers and employees and the second is guaranteeing a return on investment.

Having worked extensively across the UK, Europe and Australia, I specialise in getting the best out of managers and all levels of employees, this has resulted in The Psychology of Leadership Mastery which ensures you do not fall down the mountain on any of the:

HOW TO AVOID THE 17½ ROUTES
TO INEFFECTIVE LEADERSHIP

Last year I conducted more than 125 seminars and speeches across a wide spectrum of business.

The topics covered in those seminars.

Included the:

- 3 elements of true motivation
- 4 principles of maintaining momentum
- 6 step system for achieving a leadership mastery mindset
- 7 keys to building and maintaining relationships.

The mindset system taught in the leadership programme has been tried tested and proven by 1233 of the world's most successful business leaders.

"Human behaviour flows from three main sources: desire, emotion, and knowledge."
~ Plato ~

"The improvement of understanding is for two ends: first, our own increase of knowledge; secondly, to enable us to deliver that knowledge to others."
~ John Locke ~

"Those people who develop the ability to continuously acquire new and better forms of knowledge that they can apply to their work and to their lives will be the movers and shakers in our society for the indefinite future."
~ Brian Tracy ~

"Most of what we call management consists of making it difficult for people to get their work done."
~ Peter Drucker ~

"Innovation distinguishes between a leader and a follower."
~ Steve Jobs ~

"It usually takes me more than three weeks to prepare a good impromptu speech."
~ Mark Twain ~

"Most of the important things in the world have been accomplished by people who have kept on trying when there seemed to be no hope at all."
~ Dale Carnegie ~

"If your actions inspire others to dream more, learn more, do more and become more, you are a leader."
~ John Adam ~

"If you pick the right people and give them the opportunity to spread their wings you almost don't have to manage them."
~ Jack Welch ~

"No institution can possibly survive if it needs geniuses or supermen to manage it. It must be organized in such a way as to be able to get along under a leadership composed of average human beings."
~ Peter Drucker ~

"Great leaders are almost always great simplifiers, who can cut through argument, debate and doubt to offer a solution everybody can understand."
~ General Colin Powell ~

"We have to learn to be our own best friends because we fall too easily into the trap of being our own worst enemies."
~ Roderick Thorp ~

HOW TO AVOID THE 17½ ROUTES
TO INEFFECTIVE LEADERSHIP

◘ RULE ONE:
ME, MYSELF AND I

To avoid creating excellence within people, training must always be about the trainer's knowledge and how intelligent they are. The leader / manager or trainer must ensure that the participants leave the session feeling inferior and with their self esteem stripped away.

Ensure that the participants feel grateful you allowed them into your training sessions. This will ensure that their self-esteem and self-efficacy are stripped away.

Or you could...

Follow the advice of Psychologist Professor Albert Bandura: *"In order to succeed, people need a sense of self-efficacy, to struggle together with resilience to meet the inevitable obstacles of life. If self-esteem and self –efficacy are lacking, people tend to behave ineffectually even though they know what to do"*

What great words of wisdom, as a leader you must build not destroy self-esteem.

> # Psychologists confirm that
> # "WE CANNOT CONSISTENTLY OUT PERFORM THE IMAGE WE HAVE OF OURSELVES"

It is estimated the cost to UK businesses by employees being disengaged from their work is £175 BILLION

87% of employees in a recent survey said that there is significantly more they could do in their job.

The key words in that last statement are: "significantly more" not just a little bit more but significantly more. The question I need to ask you is this "What is this costing your business?"

WE GENERALLY CHANGE OURSELVES FOR ONE OF TWO REASONS.: INSPIRATION OR DESPERATION

Understanding how to build self-esteem and confidence is vital if knowledge is to be turned into positive action. Remember you cannot succeed by yourself. It's hard to find a rich hermit.

> # Creating Excellence Within People is a skill that can be learnt and transferred to every member of your team!

HOW TO AVOID THE 17½ ROUTES
TO INEFFECTIVE LEADERSHIP

◘ RULE TWO:
C.R.E.W.

Training that encourages a growth within participants in any of the following areas must be banned from the syllabus

◘ ◘

Confidence

Respect

Efficacy

Worthiness

The four elements mentioned above are the corner stones of creating excellence within people

Confidence: People are afraid to even try or suggest something new when they lack confidence; how many great profit making or cost cutting ideas have gone unsaid in your business?

Respect: you have to have it first in order to give it to others i.e. your customers and fellow employees. If you don't respect yourself you will never respect the customers or other employees

Low Efficacy: levels will result in an employee who never thinks for themselves, offer solutions and will resist any form of change. They contribute very little to your bottom line profit.

Worthiness: is having a sense of pride in your work not for the bosses' sake but for their own sense of pride and worthiness.

Or you could…

Create a team of employees that are all pulling together, look how successful Sir Steve Redgrave and his team have been; every employee has the potential to increase their levels of confidence, respect for themselves and others, their levels of self efficacy and a feeling of worthiness

I recently employed several local tradesmen to build an extension to my office. They each worked with a sense of self worthiness and pride. They also constantly thought ahead to the other trades that need to install electrics or plumbing. Their sense of worthiness saved me a considerable sum of time and money by not having to redo things that had just been done.

> ## Getting it right first time is always more profitable than having to redo, re-send or refund

Ensure your training measures all for aspects of CREW before and after training.

A proven technique that allows a person to develop a greater sense of personal Confidence, Respect, Efficacy and

Worthiness is to give them precise feedback and to involve them in that feedback by encouraging them reflect and comment on how they would improve the outcome next time.

Precise feedback is proven to be five times more effective.

> ## "It is knowing how to be different that makes the difference"

"I CAN is 100 times more important than IQ",
~ Author Unknown ~

*"I was always looking outside myself for strength and confidence but it comes from within.
It is there all the time."*
~ Anna Freud ~

*"And what, Socrates, is the food of the soul?
Surely, I said, knowledge is the food of the soul."*
~ Plato ~

"If you don't design your own life plan, chances are you'll fall into someone else's plan, and guess what they have planned for you? Not much."
~ Jim Rohn ~

"Someone's opinion of you does not have to become your reality."
~ Les Brown ~

"Trust yourself. Create the kind of self that you will be happy to live with all your life. Make the most of yourself by fanning the tiny, inner sparks of possibility into flames of achievement."
~ Golda Meir ~

"The most important opinion you have is the one you have of yourself, and the most significant things you say all day are those things you say to yourself."
~ Unknown Author ~

"The majority of men meet with failure because of their lack of persistence in creating new plans to take the place of those which fail."
~ Napoleon Hill ~

HOW TO AVOID THE 17½ ROUTES
TO INEFFECTIVE LEADERSHIP

☐ RULE THREE:
TOTALLY IGNORE THE 6Ps

Proper Prior Planning Prevents Poor Performance.

Before you launch into your training, be sure to ignore all the workplace issues that can sabotage your efforts before you even begin.

Realize that much of the time, money, and resources you invest in training will be wasted if certain factors outside the training room are neglected.

Most companies fail to see the bigger picture; training is used as a sticking plaster for some of the following areas:

- Culture
- Morale
- Uncertainty of the future
- Past poor management
- Resentment

A good role model for this approach is the ostrich; just stick your head in the sand and let's pretend that our corner of the world is perfect.

Or you could...

Work with employees to re-engage

them with a positive business culture, re-engage them to take ownership of their career development, remove resentment and uncertainty.

A study of 1007 CEO's found that the number-one trait that they are looking for in 2013, for their businesses to succeed is the skill of collaboration. 75% of the CEO's said developing the skills of collaboration is critical.

◌

To develop the theme of collaboration further:

Professor TJ Stanley interviewed 733 of the world's top business owners; they listed honest communication as their number one success tip. Failing to plan is without doubt seen by employees as not only incompetence but also dishonest to them.

> *"The best preparation for tomorrow is to do today's work superbly well."*
> ~ Sir William Osler ~

How many of your employees have their heads buried in the sand. What a difference it will make to your bottom line profit when they are willing to see the light. Did you know that 72% of engaged employees believe they can positively affect customer service?

"We always plan too much and always think too little."
~ Joseph Schumper ~

"It's not the plan that is important, it's the planning."
~ Dr Graeme Edwards ~

"Planning is an unnatural process; it is much more fun to do something. The nicest thing about not planning is that failure comes as a complete surprise, rather than being preceded by a period of worry and depression."
~ Sir John Harvey-Jones ~

"Surmounting difficulty is the crucible that forms character."
~ Tony Robbins ~

REFLECTION PAGE

RULE 1

- HOW WOULD RATE YOUR OWN SELF-ESTEEM ON A SCALE OF ONE TO TEN?

- MAKE A LIST OF WHAT YOU ARE GOOD AT AND READ IT EVERY DAY

RULE 2

- IN YOUR TEAM WHO ARE THE LONE ROWERS

- WHO ARE THE TEAM PLAYERS/ ROWERS?

RULE 3

- WHERE IN YOUR BUSINESS DO YOU REGULARLY HAVE TO RE-DO, RE-SEND, REFUND?

- WHAT ACTION CAN YOU TAKE IN ORDER TO PREVENT POOR PERFORMANCE?

HOW TO AVOID THE 17½ ROUTES
TO INEFFECTIVE LEADERSHIP

◘ RULE FOUR: FEAR RULES

Human beings have a natural fear of change. Research tells us that managers who are promoted for their product knowledge more often than not have poor people skills.

Here is the classic Catch 22 situation:

> Poor People Skills Promote Fear,
> Fear Promotes Resistance To Change,
> Resistance To Change Generates Fear!

Employees are like light bulbs, they are not much good when they are turned off. Managers who have poor people skills literally turn off their staff.

Employees either quit or leave or more worryingly they quit and stay.

Failing to maximize your employees' full potential is proven to cost UK businesses £175 billion per year.

> *"Thinking will not overcome fear but action will."*
> ~ W. Clement Stone ~

Or you could…

Give managers the tools and techniques to not only improve their own performance to its full potential, but also encourage those they manage to reach their full potential.

Fear release a hormone called cortisol. Cortisol reduces our ability to think and act in a clear manner. Rule by fear and you will undoubtedly be realizing cortisol.

Compare this to creating an environment where employees feel safe to say "I don't know" or "could you explain that again please"

When a person feels happy and safe they release noradrenaline, which is a feel good hormone which makes us feel good about ourselves, good about the job I am doing. Noradrenalin also helps us to focus

> *"The greatest discovery of my generation is that human beings can alter their lives by altering their attitude of mind."*
> ~ William James Psychologist ~

RULE FIVE: JUST ADD WATER / RIDICULE TRAINEES

You must pressure employees to emerge from the training session with at least 20 years of instant experience.

Ignore the understanding that "learning" needs a little time to fully integrate into new behaviour and actions; using ridicule and pressure as a technique will result in the employee going back into old patterns and habits they have been comfortable in.

This will ensure that your budget and time invested has been truly wasted.

'If left to its own devices retention of learning drops dramatically within 48 hours and continues to drop every day.'

Or you could:

We have all met in our lives people who use words as a way of putting people down. We all know how it makes us feel when we hear it.

Compare these two quotes

> *"Blowing out another person's candle will not make yours burn brighter."*
>
> ~~~
>
> *"A thousand candles can be lighted from the flame of one candle, and the life of the candle will not be shortened. Happiness can be spread without diminishing that of your-self."*
> ~ Mahatma Gandhi ~

Make sure you are lighting candles not blowing them out?

Remember you are either building self-esteem or you are destroying it.

"The task of the leader is to get his people from where they are to where they have not been."
~ Henry Kissinger ~

"Leaders must be close enough to relate to others, but far enough ahead to motivate them."
~ John C. Maxwell ~

When spider webs unite, they can tie up a lion."
~ Ethiopian Proverb ~

"When was ever honey made with one bee in a hive?"
~ Thomas Hood ~

"The task of leadership is not to put greatness into humanity, but to elicit it, for the greatness is already there."
~ John Buchan ~

"Success is nothing more than a few simple disciplines, practiced every day."
~ Jim Rohn ~

Adapted from
~ Dorothy Law Nolte and Rachel Harris ~

IF

If employees work with criticism, they learn to condemn.

If employees work with hostility, they learn to fight.

If employees work with fear, they learn to be apprehensive.

If employees work with pity, they learn to
feel sorry for themselves.

If employees work with ridicule, they learn to feel shy.

If employees work with jealousy, they learn to feel envy.

If employees work with shame, they learn to feel guilty.

If employees work with encouragement,
they learn confidence.

If employees work with tolerance, they learn patience.

If employees work with praise, they learn appreciation.

If employees work with acceptance, they learn to love.

If employees work with approval, they learn
to like themselves.

*If employees work with recognition, they learn
it is good to have a goal.*

If employees work with sharing, they learn generosity.

If employees work with honesty, they learn truthfulness.

If employees work with fairness, they learn justice.

*If employees work with kindness and consideration,
they learn respect.*

*If employees work with security, they learn to have
faith in themselves and in those about them.*

*If employees work with friendliness, they learn
the world is a nice place in which to live.*

REFLECTION PAGE

RULE 4

- DO YOU OR THOSE YOU MANAGE FEEL SAFE TO EXPRESS IDEAS AND OPINIONS?

RULE 5

- WHAT ACTIONS DO YOU NEED TO STOP BLOWING OUT PEOPLES CANDLES?
- WHAT MORE COULD YOU DO TO LIGHT PEOPLES CANDLES?

◘ RULE SIX:
NEVER BALANCE YOUR COMPANY'S VISIONS AND VALUES WITH THOSE OF THE TRAINING COMPANIES

Use external seminars for training that are not supportive or reflective of your organizational priorities, goals, expectations, messages and behaviours.

'Off' the shelf" training is proven to be 37% successful. Buying "off the shelf" programmes that do not incorporate your unique environment, language, expectations, culture and priorities will fail.

You can guarantee **NOT** to expect dramatic results from a one size fits all approach.

Or you could:

Increase your success rate substantially if the training aligns both your vision with values. Both the vision and the values set by a company must blend with those who attend the training. Values are the cement that binds a company together.

If your employees do not know or subscribe to your values there will always be a discord.

REFLECTIONS PAGE

- HOW BESPOKE IS YOUR CURRENT TRAINING?
- WHAT IS YOUR VISION FOR THE FUTURE?
- WHAT ARE YOUR MUST HAVE VALUES?

HOW TO AVOID THE 17½ ROUTES
TO INEFFECTIVE LEADERSHIP

▢ RULE SEVEN:
THE MUSHROOM THEORY

Keep your employees in the dark; do not tell them anything about the training or anything else that is important, simply order them to turn up.

This ensures that the employee attends the session because they are told to, not because they are genuinely inspired to.

The employee's supervisor must not prepare them or participate in the follow up to reinforce what has been learnt.

Abdicate this accountability to the person doing the training.

A proven technique to ensure failure is to only tell those attending the training 5 minutes before the session begins. This will guarantee they are totally stressed, angry, frustrated and feel that the work they intended to do that day has very little value.

Or you could...

Guarantees employees receive a clear understand of the training outcomes and how it will help them to work either easier with less stress hassle and frustration or equally how it will help their career.

This ensures they are fully prepared to implement strategies that are clear and encourage employees to maximize their own true potential and the true potential of those they manage.

It is psychologically proven that when employees are involved, inspired and ignited into a project or task they will produce results far in excess of employees who are kept in the dark and fed poor information

> *"If you don't like how things are, change it!*
> *You're not a tree."*
> ~ Jim Rohn ~
>
> *"The winner's edge is not in a gifted birth, a high IQ, or in talent. The winner's edge is all in the attitude, not aptitude. Attitude is the criterion for success."*
> ~ Dennis Waitley ~

◘ RULE EIGHT:
IGNORE ALL THE SIGNS

Use any form of training to cover the real problems. It does not matter that the training is not relevant to solving thorny and often complex issues that encourage poor role clarity.

Unclear performance expectations, vague job descriptions, poor or inconsistent performance are ignored.

You must ignore the real issues and then blame the training. This rule is an extension to rule seven - The Mushroom Theory.

If your goal is to fail you must not set clear guidelines of what is expected of your employees. Let them guess what is expected of them and then reprimand them for guessing wrong.

Or you could...

Help establish a management culture where the directions, role clarity, performance expectations and job descriptions are visible for all to see and poor or inconsistent performance will be the eliminated.

> ## Research shows that only 29% of employees are actively engaged in their jobs.

These are employees who work with passion and a feeling that they are connected to their company. People that are actively engaged help move the organization forward.

Maximizing your employees' full potential is a proven method of raising bottom line profit at no extra production costs.

Helping people to be the best they can be is one of the most productive methods of increasing bottom line profit at no extra production costs

> *"People don't resist change. They resist being changed!"*
> ~ Peter Senge ~
>
> *"Knowledge which is acquired under compulsion obtains no hold on the mind."*
> ~ Plato ~

HOW TO AVOID THE 17½ ROUTES
TO INEFFECTIVE LEADERSHIP

◘ RULE NINE: NEVER MEASURE THE EFFECTIVENESS' OF THE TRAINING

The key things that need improvement are **NOT** to be adequately measured before or after the training. Skills, knowledge, behaviours, service levels, sales, and/or culture must be treated as if the training never happened.

Always remember, if it is not measured you cannot be responsible.

> *"The best measure of a man's honesty isn't his income tax return. It's the zero adjust on his bathroom scale."*
> ~ Arthur C. Clarke ~
>
> *"Action is the real measure of intelligence."*
> ~ Napoleon Hill ~

Or you could...

Measure the before and after scores of the training ensuring an excellent return on your investment

If you are looking to improve behaviour, moral and connectedness then measure both Emotional intelligence and self-esteem before and after the training.

Link this with a personal development plan and you have a formula for success.

"I think that the best training a top manager can be engaged in is management by example. I want to make sure there is no discrepancy between what we say and what we do. If you preach accountability and then promote somebody with bad results, it doesn't work. I personally believe the best development is management by example. Don't believe what I say. Believe what I do."
~ Carlos Ghosn, CEO of Renault-Nissan ~

HOW TO AVOID THE 17½ ROUTES
TO INEFFECTIVE LEADERSHIP

◘ RULE TEN:
NEVER RE-EVALUATE PERFORMANCE EXPECTATIONS

You must never inform trainees they have made improvements or shown new levels of skill. See rule nine.

The training must be provided without corresponding changes in performance expectations or performance reviews. This allows for diminished accountability and will continue to compromise long term results.

You are not in business to pamper to peoples wounded egos. Derren Brown has made a fortune from mind reading, so let them read your mind if they need to know how they are doing.

> *"Culture does not change because we desire to change it. Culture changes when the organization is transformed; the culture reflects the realities of people working together every day."*
> ~ Frances Hesselbein ~

Or you could...

To show managers how to praise or reprimand staff in less than 60 seconds. A technique that is tried, tested and proven to be 5 times more effective than the ones they are using now.

The psychology of achievement shows leaders how to get the best out of people in the shortest possible time, and the most productive outcome for all concerned.

An example of feedback could be "thanks for today, good night" Or you could say:

Thank you for getting those orders out on time, the customer was extremely grateful when I spoke with them earlier"

Has your previous training given you a great return on your investment?

Based on what you have read so far has your previous training embraced the key success point raised so far?

> "Time is more value than money. You can get more money, but you cannot get more time."
> ~ Jim Rohn ~

HOW TO AVOID THE 17½ ROUTES
TO INEFFECTIVE LEADERSHIP

☐ RULE ELEVEN: THE GUESSING GAME

Never tell your employees your desired outcome; keep them on a need to know rule. After all what do they know that we lofty managers could possible benefit from?

Always remain unclear or non-specific about your expectations delivered in team meetings, staff forums and/or training sessions. It's important **NOT** to state clearly, consistently and frequently, "We will support you and expect you to do things differently after the training"

> "If speaking is silver, then listening is gold."
> ~ Turkish Proverb ~
>
> "If there is any great secret of success in life, it lies in the ability to put yourself in the other person's place and to see things from his point of view - as well as your own."
> ~ Henry Ford ~

Or you could...

Benefit from the research that has proven employees who are most committed perform 20% better and are 87% less likely to leave the organization. One of the top reasons for employees leaving a company is "not feeling valued".

Communication or a lack of it is estimated to be 93 % of the cause of conflict and poor relationships.

Understanding the power of communication is vital, take a look at these research findings:

> ## The power of communication is in using Sensory Based Language

Percentage of the population who are
Visual 35%
Auditory 25%
Kinaesthetic 40%

Being able to read a person's language and then respond in their sensory based language will help build rapport and a deeper understanding.

> *"Seek first to understand and then to be understood."*
> ~ Stephen Covey ~

Psychologist have calculated that during an average conversation a person pays attention to the following

7% is the WORDS we use, while

38% of the conversation we are paying attention to the TONE

55% of the conversation is how we interpret BODY LANGUAGE

> *"To solve any problem, here are three questions to ask yourself: First, what could I do? Second, what could I read? And third, who could I ask?"*
> ~ Jim Rohn ~
>
> *"Look at a day when you are supremely satisfied at the end. It's not a day when you lounge around doing nothing; it's when you've had everything to do, and you've done it."*
> ~ Margaret Thatcher ~

REFLECTION PAGE

RULE 7

- HOW GOOD ARE YOU / YOUR TEAM AT EXPLAINING AND DELIVERING DESIRED OUTCOMES?

RULE 8

- REFLECT ON THE TWO QUOTES ON PAGE 50

> *"People don't resist change. They resist being changed!"*
> ~ Peter Senge ~
>
> *"Knowledge which is acquired under compulsion obtains no hold on the mind."*
> ~ Plato ~

RULE 9

- WITH YOUR CURRENT TRAINING WHAT ARE YOU MEASURING?

RULE 10

- BECAUSE FEEDBACK IS KING; WHEN DID YOU LAST PURPOSEFULLY GIVE FEEDBACK?

RULE 11

- DID YOU KNOW THE PERCENTAGES OF THE POPULATION THAT ARE:

  VISUAL
  AUDITORY
  KINAESTHETIC

- IF NOT WHAT ELSE ARE YOU AND YOUR TEAM MISSING OUT ON THAT WOULD GIVE THEM THE EDGE OVER YOUR COMPETITORS?

HOW TO AVOID THE 17½ ROUTES
TO INEFFECTIVE LEADERSHIP

◻ RULE TWELVE: DEATH BY POWER POINT

Using fellow employees or inexperienced trainers is a great way for the training to fail.

You want your trainer to be able to bore your employees in the morning and not just straight after lunch.

The training should start late and finish even later than planned; after all the trainers possible do not have children to pick up from school or another meeting to go to, so what does it matter if we over run?

The trainer should know nothing about sustained levels of interest or how long it is before trainees become bored and switch off.

Trainers must be able to read from a power point slide show, with a minimum of 135 slides per hour.

Participants must not be allowed to ask questions of the trainer as this takes up valuable time and may inadvertently be of some benefit.

Or allow one participant to dominate all interaction.

Allowing this participant to inflate their ego in front of the other students is more important than the training content.

> *"Perhaps the world's second worst crime is boredom. The first is being a bore."*
> ~ Cecil Beaton ~
>
> *"To err is human, but to really foul things up you need a computer."*
> ~ Paul Ehrlich ~
>
> *"I saw a subliminal advertising executive, but only for a second."*
> ~ Steven Wright ~

Or you could…

Guarantee success and use a trainer that is enthusiastic, credible, experienced and comfortable in even the most challenging group environments.

Involve, Inspire and Ignite. These are the three key factors that will fully engage your staff and allow them to become more productive. To ensure fully engaged employees training needs to be fun, interactive and memorable and more importantly it need to engage the participants.

Research by Watson Wyatt interviewed over 8,500 private sector workers from across Europe and found the following levels of employees that described themselves as "fully engaged"

- **36%** of Swiss,
- **24%** of Irish
- **18%** of German employees.
- **12% of UK employees could be described as "fully engaged"**

- Only Italian employees, at **9%,** were less engaged than the UK

What is this costing your business?

REFLECTION PAGE

RULE 12

- IF YOU WERE TO RE-EXAMINE ONE OF YOUR POWERPOINT PRESENTATIONS
- WHAT PERCENTAGE WOULD BE WORDS
- WHAT PERCENTAGE WOULD BE IMAGES?
- HOW MUCH UNNECESSARY INFORMATION DID YOU HAVE ON EACH SLIDE?

HOW TO AVOID THE 17½ ROUTES
TO INEFFECTIVE LEADERSHIP

☐ RULE THIRTEEN: 13 UNLUCKY FOR SOME

You do not have to work hard to fail in Leadership. Research informs us that 87% of employees have switched off within six months of joining a company.

Applying the rules you have learnt so far will ensure one of two things

1. If I was not switched off before, I am now.
2. If I was switched off before, I am now convinced that I was right to switch off.
3. **Remember only 12% of UK employees could be described as "fully engaged.** Only Italian employees, at 9%, were less engaged than the UK.

> "Success or failure in business is caused more by the mental attitude even than by mental capacities."
> ~ Walter Scott ~

Or you could…

Train your manager's leaders and supervisors ways of switching employees back on and that would be a great return on investment, even better is the fact that prevention is far better than cure.

Therefore it must be easier to communicate the points covered so far in this book and engage with your employees. This is prevention of them switching off rather than having to switch them back on again.

> **How is your bottom line profit being affected if only 13% of your employees are switched on?**

> *"In everyone's life, at some time, our inner fire goes out. It is then burst into flame by an encounter with another human being. We should all be thankful for those people who rekindle the inner spirit."*
> ~ Albert Schweitzer ~

> *"What man actually needs is not a tensionless state but rather the striving and struggling for some goal worthy of him. What he needs is not the discharge of tension at any cost, but the call of a potential meaning waiting to be fulfilled by him."*
> ~ Victor Frankl ~

HOW TO AVOID THE 17½ ROUTES
TO INEFFECTIVE LEADERSHIP

◘ RULE FOURTEEN: RETURN ON INVESTMENT

Save money by using nonqualified trainers. This is an extremely useful method in wasting your budget.

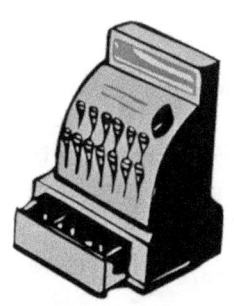

How hard can it be stand in front of people and talk? Just ask Gerald Ratner, he achieved notoriety after making a speech in which he jokingly denigrated the company's products, almost singlehandedly causing the company to collapse.

What possible negative impact can it have on results such as?

- Sales
- Increase or maintain profit
- Retention and image
- Performance
- Employee loyalty/trust
- Maintain relationships
- Building customer loyalty/trust
- Customer service
- Fostering teamwork

Or you could...

There is no substitute to using a qualified profession tutor who would fully understand your desired outcome, know how to involve, inspire and ignite employees

> **Extensive research has shown that MENTORING PROGRAMMES yields a significantly higher return on investment.**

Ensuring you will see the

- Increase in sales
- Increase in profit
- Improved retention and image
- Improved performance
- Building of employee loyalty/trust
- Start or maintenance of positive relationships
- Increase in customer loyalty/trust
- Improved customer service
- Fostering of teamwork
- Creation of new areas for business growth.

"Management is efficiency in climbing the ladder of success; leadership determines whether the ladder is leaning against the right wall."
~ Stephen R. Covey ~

Employees who are most committed perform 20% better and are 87% less likely to leave the organization

The estimated cost of losing a manager is in excess of £65,000

Effective Leadership Mastery creates employees who:

- Are passionate about their work
- Want to take ownership and responsibility for the success of your company
- See their work as being worthwhile
- Have a clear understanding of the bigger picture
- Go the extra mile, not because you ask them to, but because they want to
- Are focused on delivering excellence for what they see as both yours and their customer's interests.
- Understand the importance of customers' satisfaction
- Are proud of their work
- Believe in your company's vision and values
- See themselves as a business owner, rather than an employee.

> "If your job was to travel to the moon, how soon would you need to know you were off course?

"It is the job of a leader to keep employees on course and stop them from missing their targets"

"The mind, once expanded to the dimensions of larger ideas, never returns to its original size."
~ Oliver W. Holmes ~

"Minds are like parachutes, they only function when they are open."
~ Sir James Dewar ~

"An idea is never given to you without you being given the power to make it reality. You must, nevertheless, suffer for it."
~ Richard Bach ~

"Information is the seed for an idea, and only grows when it's watered."
~ Heinz V. Bergen ~

RULE FIFTEEN: THE PRINCIPLES OF INFLUENCE

The art of influence is a proven science that can be learnt; ensuring that manager's leaders and supervisors are ignorant of these principles automatically ensures that Leadership Mastery will be doomed to fail.

Or you could:

Through the process of influence we generate and manage change.

Change must be fully accepted and successfully implemented for it to be lasting.

As such, it is important for those wishing to create and sustain practical change to understand fully the workings of the influence process.

Fortunately, a vast body of scientific evidence now exists on how, when, and why people say yes to influence attempts.

The Six Principles of influence were created by Professor of Psychology Robert Cialdini, He published them in his respected book "Influence: The Psychology of Persuasion."

- Reciprocity
- Commitment and Consistency
- Social Proof
- Authority
- Liking
- Scarcity

Influencing others is challenging, which is why it's worth understanding the psychological principles behind the influencing process.

Cialdini identified the six principles through experimental studies, and by immersing himself in the world of what he called "compliance professionals" – salespeople, fund raisers, recruiters, advertisers, marketers, and so on. These are people skilled in the art of convincing and influencing others.

These principles are so powerful that they generate desirable change in the all areas of business

> *"An ounce of action is worth a ton of theory."*
> ~ Friedrich Engels ~

HOW TO AVOID THE 17½ ROUTES TO INEFFECTIVE LEADERSHIP

◘ RULE SIXTEEN: AVOID THE FRANK SINATRA PRINCIPLE

One very successful method of wasting your valuable time is to have one un-qualified person do all of your employee engagement. This technique is very useful for occupying all your time and not being very productive.

Or you could:

Use the Frank Sinatra principle,

Frank Sinatra specialized in singing and entertaining from stage, he did not design the posters, print the tickets, stand in the box office and sell the tickets. He did not take your hat and coat as you entered the theatre. What he did was what he was exceptionally good at performing, singing and entertaining.

Learning the skills of prioritizing and having the skills of delegation provides the know how that increases performance, allowing you to do the job you are more skilled, and productive at. What could you achieve if you had more time?

REFLECTION PAGE

RULE 13

- WHAT PERCENTAGE OF YOUR TEAM HAVE SWITCHED OFF?
- WHO HAS QUIT AND STAYED?

RULE 14

- WHY NOT SAMPLE THE PSYCHOLOGY OF LEADERSHIP MASTERY'S

  "EVERYTHING I LEARNT ABOUT LEADERSHIP I LEARNT FROM A PINEAPPLE: 9½ REFRESHING LEADERSHIP FACTS" OVER A WORKING LUNCH OR EARLY MORNING MEETING.

  IF YOU ARE NOT 100% SATISFIED, EXCITED, INVOLVED AND INSPIRED THERE IS NO CHARGE FOR MY TIME.

RULE 15

- UNDERSTANDING THESE LAWS IS A MUST FOR EVERY SALES TEAM OR CUSTOMER FACING EMPLOYEE.

RULE 16

- WHERE ARE YOU BEING FRANK SINATRA?

HOW TO AVOID THE 17½ ROUTES
TO INEFFECTIVE LEADERSHIP

☐ RULE SEVENTEEN: THE LAWS OF SUCCESSFUL PEOPLE

I encourage you to not discover the laws of success. Should you inadvertently apply these rules to your business, you could singlehandedly fail in your desire to keep working longer hours for longer years before having to retire on ill health or the business goes bust.

This one law alone could cause your company to

- Increase sales
- Increase profit
- Improve retention and image
- Improve performance
- Build employee loyalty/trust
- Build customer loyalty/trust
- Improve customer service
- Fostering teamwork
- Reduce costs

Or you could...

The Psychology of Leadership Mastery Programme will give you the map

For leadership success in simple, easy to implement steps

Discover the:

- 3 elements to true motivation.
- 4 principles of maintaining momentum.
- 6 step simple system for achieving a leadership success mind set.
- 7 keys to building and maintaining relationships.

The mind-set system taught in the Leadership Mastery Programme has been tried tested and proven by 1,233 of the world's most successful business leaders. Transforming this knowledge into positive action is guaranteed to increase your business success.

If you would like a free copy of "People know what to do so why the hell don't they do it"

**please email:
john@leadershipmastery.co.uk**

REFLECTION PAGE

- IF YOU ARE NOT FAMILIAR WITH THE ABOVE POINTS WHAT COULD IT BE COSTING YOUR BUSINESS?

HOW TO AVOID THE 17½ ROUTES
TO INEFFECTIVE LEADERSHIP

◘ RULE 17½:
DO EVERYTHING
BY HALF

Developing a half-hearted attitude should be the perfect way to completely close either your department or the business itself.

Allow all employees and customers to feel they are nothing more than an annoying interruption to your day.

Use half the day to surf the internet and updating your Facebook account, while tweeting to the world what you will be having for lunch.

Extend the break times. That way you only have to produce half of the work needed

> *"Procrastination is suicide on the installment plan."*
> ~ Author Unknown ~
>
> *"The lazier a man is, the more he plans to do tomorrow."*
> ~ Norwegian Proverb ~

"Laziness is nothing more than the habit of resting before you get tired."
~ Mortimer Caplan ~

"The laziest man I ever met put popcorn in his pancakes so they would turn over by themselves."
~ W.C. Fields ~

"Too many young people itch for what they want without scratching for it."
~ Thomas Taylor ~

"Tomorrow is the only day in the year that appeals to a lazy man.
~ Jimmy Lyons ~

"Offer the lazy an egg, and they'll want you to peel it for them".
~ A Proverb ~

"There are no lazy veteran lion hunters."
~ Norman Augustine ~

REFLECTION

- WHO ARE THE HALFERS IN YOUR BUSINESS?
- WHAT CAN YOU DO TO GET THEM TO PERFORM TO THE BEST OF THEIR ABILITY?

The following poem reflects the consequences of doing things by half.

THE MAN IN THE MIRROR

If you get what you want in
your struggle for self
And the world makes you king for a day
Then go to the mirror and look at yourself
And see what that man has to say

For it isn't a man's father, mother or wife
whose judgment upon him must pass
the fellow whose verdict counts
Most in his life
is the man staring back from the glass

He's the fellow to please, never mind the rest
for he's with you clear up to the end
and you've passed your most
dangerous, difficult test
If the man in the glass is your friend

You can fool the whole world
down the pathway of years
And get pats on the back as you pass
But your final reward will be
heartache and tears
If you've cheated the man in the glass

Dale Wimbrow

Or you could:

TRANSFORM KNOWLEDGE
IN 2 POSITIVE ACTION

Applying the principles in this book will encourage participants to buy in to The Psychology of Leadership Mastery for their benefit as well as the company's. The programme uses a specially designed consultation technique, participants see for themselves the impact their old half hearted attitude is having on themselves.

> *"If you think you are too small to have an impact try going to bed with a mosquito in the room."*
> ~ Author Unknown ~
>
> *"I can't imagine a person becoming a success who doesn't give this game of life everything he's got."*
> ~ Walter Cronkite ~
>
> *"In everyone's life, at some time, our inner fire goes out. It is then burst into flame by an encounter with another human being. We should all be thankful for those people who rekindle the inner spirit."*
> ~ Albert Schweitzer ~

THE FOUR STEPS TO SUCCESS

4 simple steps:

STEP 1: Know What You Want

STEP 2: Turn Knowledge into Action

STEP 3: Notice What's Working and Not Working

STEP 4: Change Your Approach and Try Again

it's that simple. Now you may want to argue that it's not that easy, but easy or not... it is that simple.

Everyone seems to get stuck on a different step.

STEP 1 is probably the biggest obstacle for people. Most people have never really thought about what they want from their career, their life

Since you're reading this and seeking information on how to improve the productivity of your career / business. I will assume that you've just completed Step 1

So let's talk about

STEP 2 : Take Action.

Here's what Action is not. It's not ordering books and audio courses.

That's learning and education.

Now while that is essential to your business success, it does not count as action. Sorry. Here's what does count as action:

Pick up the phone now to discuss how The Psychology of Leadership Mastery Can help you achieve your desired outcomes. 01224 548 814

> *"The way to get started is to quit talking and begin doing."*
> ~ Walt Disney ~
>
> *"WE CAN'T SOLVE PROBLEMS BY USING THE SAME KIND OF THINKING WE USED WHEN WE CREATED THEM."*
> ~ Albert Einstein ~
>
> *"WE CANNOT CONSISTENTLY OUT PERFORM THE IMAGE WE HAVE OF OURSELVES."*
> ~ Dr, J Brothers ~
>
> *"The secret of success is constancy to purpose."*
> ~ Benjamin Disraeli ~

STEP 3: Notice What's Working and Not Working

Using the latest psychologically tried tested and proven techniques and over 24 years' practical experience to figure out What's Working and Not Working, The Psychology of Leadership Mastery outcomes are guaranteed to succeed.

> "Making your mark on the world is hard. If it were easy, everybody would do it. But it's not. It takes patience, it takes commitment, and it comes with plenty of failure along the way. The real test is not whether you avoid this failure, because you won't. it's whether you let it harden or shame you into inaction, or whether you learn from it; whether you choose to persevere."
> ~ Barack Obama ~
>
> "Most of the important things in the world have been accomplished by people who have kept on trying when there seemed to be no hope at all."
> ~ Dale Carnegie ~

STEP 4: Change Your Approach and Try Something Different

So save yourself 20 plus years and take my word on this one because

"IT IS KNOWING HOW TO BE DIFFERENT THAT MAKES THE DIFFERENCE"

THE PSYCHOLOGY OF LEADERSHIP MASTERY

Knows the proven ways of how to make the difference to your training and development, the people that succeed in this world are the ones that are not afraid to change and try something different

> *"What man actually needs are not a tensionless state but rather the striving and struggling for some goal worthy of him. What he needs is not the discharge of tension at any cost, but the call of a potential meaning waiting to be fulfilled by him."*
> ~ Victor Frankl ~

More Success, More Easily & More Often

Take the 8 minute leadership success profile.

Our leadership success profile measures the top 5 qualities measured against 16,222 successful leaders in order of importance and then compares them to your individual manager or leader, giving you and them a complete measurable blueprint for development and success.

Here at The Psychology of Leadership Mastery we are the only UK Company offering a Transforming Knowledge into Positive Action Guarantee.

◻ **Failure is not an option... because we offer a 100% satisfaction guarantee**

If after implementing and using the tried, tested and proven strategies that you will learn you do not see the knowledge turned into actionable results we will give you a refund

We are the only UK Company offering a Knowledge into Action guarantee

Ebbinghaus curve

Professor Hermann Ebbinghaus did a series of experiments related to how we learn and retain information, his results are widely accepted as a general theory for how we learn and retain information.

Graphing his results, he developed a formula for how long items remain in our memory. Some people may remember better than others, but the general trend for how long we retain information is the same.

The resulting graph is called **Ebbinghaus' Forgetting Curve.** The bad news is, it's steeper than you may think. The good news is, there are strategies you can use to improve your memory retention.

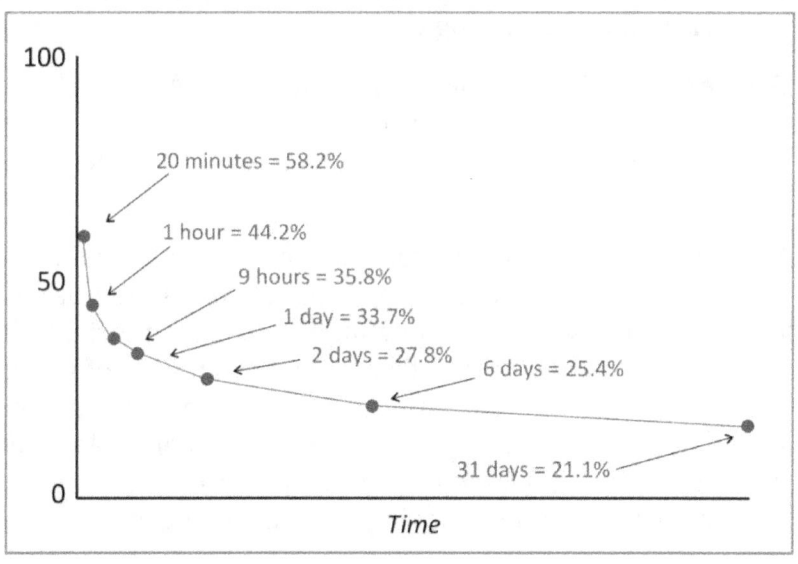

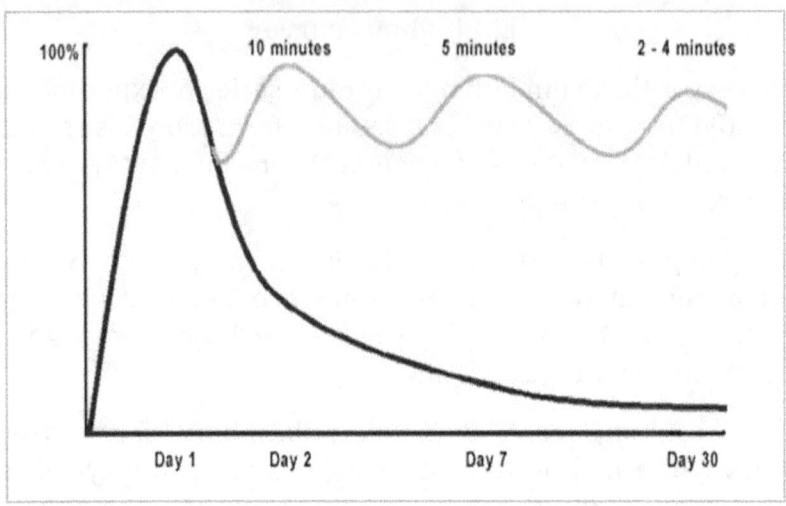

Participants who spend **10 minutes reviewing information within 24 hours of receiving will raise the curve almost to 100% again.**

A week later, it only takes 5 minutes to "reactivate" the same material and again raise the curve. By day 30, your brain will only need 2-4 minutes to give you the feedback, "Yes, I know that…"

So how do we help them overcome the Ebbinghaus Curve? Well the speed of forgetting depends on a number of factors such as the meaningfulness of the information, stress level, repetition of information and the use of whole brain learning. I recently ran a mentoring programme for one of the UK's largest employers the General Manager summed up the effectiveness of my sessions by saying "all my managers are now speaking the same language."

A better approach for long term retention is to focus on the quality of the information represented in memory and the meaning of the information to you. In plain English:

If you learn something, and it is important to you, and you can connect it with many things you already know, your memory retention will be very high

If you learn something, and it is **not** important to you, and you **do not** connect it with anything you already know, you will have poor retention and require regular repetition

This is why change is rarely permanent and will evaporate over time. it is easy to forget if we do nothing to fit it in the mind.

The Psychology of Leadership Mastery is founded on the principle of understanding both the mind and our behaviour in order to create lasting positive change.

SUCCESS STORIES

"The training by John proved to be extremely insightful, fun, practical, and importantly we observed positive changes in behaviour almost immediately as a result of the training. It created a common language."

**Derek Richardson,
General Manager for Openreach BT in the North East a Cumbria**

"John Edington gave us the benefit of his considerable experience and working knowledge to help busy professionals cope with the everyday pressures of business. The feedback we received was tremendous and many of those present at our two seminars have advised that they are already using his techniques that he passed on to great effect. It's probable that most people have never been tutored on how to use the mind to best effect, and we will most definitely ask John to give us more excellent guidance."

**Alan Cowie,
Director Hunter Cowie**

"This mentoring programme came at a critical time in my business life. It was a gift of opportunity and support. Full of insight and inspiration, I felt empowered throughout the whole process."

SJG Managing Director

"John, Many thanks again for the session: The word that resonates for me is 'profound'. "

CB Global Sales Manager

SUMMARY OF THE RULES

Rule One

Understand the importance of building self esteem and confidence if knowledge is to be turned into action.

Shame based development and learning is totally counter productive

Rule Two

The Psychology of Leadership Mastery encourages a growth within participants in any of the following areas:

Confidence

Respect

Efficacy

Worthiness

Rule Three

Any form of training and development is affected by past and current events. Addressing these issues will have a positive impact on y results.

Failing to plan is planning to fail because if you do not have a clear plan employees will feel that both you and you goal are not congruent.

Rule Four

Deal with the fear of change

Poor People Skills Promote Fear;
Fear Promotes Resistance To Change;
Resistance To Change Promotes Fear!

Rule Five

Understanding that "learning" needs a little time to fully integrate into new behaviour and actions

Rule Six

In order to be a Leadership Master you must be supportive or reflective of your organizational priorities, goals, expectations, messages and behaviours.

Buying "off the shelf" programs that do not incorporate your unique environment, language, expectations, culture and priorities are considerably less effective.

Rule Seven

Involve, inspire and ignite your employees, let them see the benefits to them of what you are offering, not just the benefits to you

Rule Eight

Help establish a management culture where the directions, role clarity, performance expectations and job descriptions are visible for all to see and poor or inconsistent performance will be eliminated.

Employee engagement is vital. These are employees who work with passion and a feeling that they are connected to their company. People that are actively engaged help move the organization forward.

Rule Nine

The key things that need improvement are adequately measured before and after the sessions:

- Skills,
- Knowledge, behaviours, service levels,
- Sales,
- Work culture.

Rule Ten

Inform trainees they have made improvements or shown new levels of skill.

The feedback must indicate and be provided with corresponding changes in performance expectations or performance reviews. This allows for accountability and will continue to improve long term results.

Rule Eleven

Tell your employees your desired outcome. Always remain clear and specific about your expectations delivered in team meetings, staff forums. It's important to state clearly, consistently and frequently, "we expect you to do things differently"

Rule Twelve

Only use a trainer that is enthusiastic, credible, experienced and comfortable in even the most challenging group environments.

Rule Thirteen

Research informs us that 87% of employees have switched off within six months of joining a company. The Psychology of Leadership Mastery is a way of switching them back on and that would be a great return on investment.

Use your The Psychology of Leadership Mastery to generate employee engagement which is critical for company growth.

Rule Fourteen

Extensive research has shown that trainers with the correct qualifications yield a higher return on investment.

Rule Fifteen

The art of influence is a proven science that can be learnt, ensuring learning encompasses these principles automatically ensures turning knowledge in2 action.

Rule Sixteen

The Frank Sinatra principle, learn the art of delegation to a qualified and experienced trainer.

Rule Seventeen

The four laws of successful people convey the message that you do not have to reinvent the wheel. Use past successes as a guide to your success

Rule Seventeen and a Half

Worthwhile Work is one of the top three reasons employees give for enjoying their work. One of the greatest rewards you can gain is the knowledge you gave it 100% and you did your best

For further information about applying:
THE PSYCHOLOGY OF LEADERSHIP MASTERY

In specific situations, such as:

- ✓ Working with a manager being groomed for promotion.
- ✓ Mentoring high performing executives whose personality styles impacts negatively on their relationship with peers, staff and clients.
- ✓ Working with executives wishing to develop their career paths and prospects.
- ✓ Mentoring as a follow up from EQ / 360-degree performance appraisals.
- ✓ Increasing the executives psychological and personal mastery skills such as self awareness, recognition of personal 'blind spots', defences and limiting thoughts, beliefs and emotional effectiveness.
- ✓ Improving the balance between work and life demands.
- ✓ Improving the executive's leadership, management and team building skills.
- ✓ Mentoring an executive to work more effectively within a changing organizational structure.
- ✓ Working with a leader to coach others in transition.
- ✓ Communication skills.
- ✓ Performance management appraisals.
- ✓ Helping the individual executive who requires new skills for a new position due to change in organizational structure.
- ✓ Developing Confidence And Self Esteem

Please contact:
JOHN EDINGTON

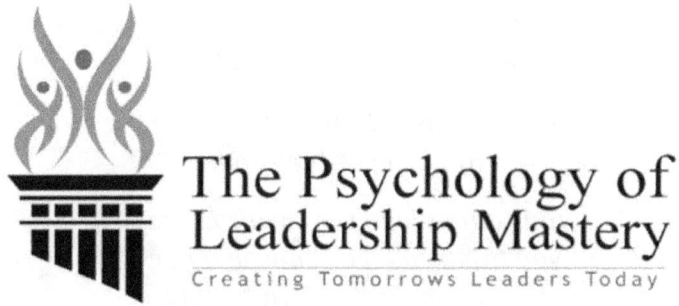

www.leadershipmastery.co.uk
Email: john@leadershipmastery.co.uk
Telephone. 01224 548 814

John Keith Edington

Author, Keynote Speaker and Broadcaster in Leadership Mastery.

Books and Training Programmes by John Edington

"How To Alienate Your Entire Workforce Faster Than Falling Off A Mountain"

"People know what to do so why the 'HELL' don't they do it?"

"You cannot lead the cavalry charge if you think you look silly on a horse"
Developing a leadership mindset

Everything I learnt About Leadership I Learnt From A Pineapple: 9½ Refreshing Leadership Facts.

THE TRUE COST OF SELF ESTEEM IN THE WORKPLACE

The results of a two year research project into identifying the financial cost of low self esteem and how to correct it.

THE ROOTS AND WINGS OF RAISING POSITIVE KIDS IN A NEGATIVE WORLD

One of my passions in life is helping children to grow into health emotionally functioning adults, while helping their parents to give their children both roots and wings.

To only dream of the person you could be is to waste the person you are.

"As a parent I have been given hundreds of articles to read concerning parenting, this book is the first that has not left me feeling guilty. The book is a positive aid to parenting; it is amazing I feel it is the best advice on parenting I have ever experienced. It was no effort to read and understand. I found the whole experience extremely helpful"

JOHN EDINGTON

Award winning motivational speaker and presenter John speaks with authority, clarity and humour.

He has a gifted ability to translate leading achievement psychological research into effortless, coherent, compelling and exciting knowledge that is instantly actionable.

His knowledge is not purely academic.

John at the top of Hellvellyn.
Nobody ever climbed a smooth mountain

He has owned and run several highly successful businesses, taking one of his businesses to a 6458% increase in turnover

John has worked extensively across the UK, Europe and Australia which has made him one of the leading speakers and most powerful professional mentor to heads of businesses, Olympic athletes and leading professionals.

Last year John conducted more than 125 seminars and speeches across a wide spectrum of both business and countries.

When he is not working, John lives with his wife in the Yorkshire Dales where his passion for his hobbies of walking and escaping to the Northumberland coast in his motor home are more than catered for.

"IT IS KNOWING HOW TO BE DIFFERENT THAT MAKES THE DIFFERENCE"

THE PSYCHOLOGY OF LEADERSHIP MASTERY

Inspires Your Employees and Customers
To Be Involved In
Igniting Your Bottom Line Profit

Vision without action is a daydream
Action without vision is a nightmare

Japanese Proverb

John Keith Edington

WHO HASN'T NEEDED A HELPING HAND NOW AND AGAIN?

I Recently I had the great pleasure of attending my niece's third birthday party at a local child friendly pub. In the manner that only a confident three year old who knows exactly what she wants, Bella ordered me to take her to play with the toys.

While she was playing I managed to park myself on a window ledge to enjoy watching the collection of children playing. At that point a little boy wobbled around the large plastic Wendy house. This little man was only just walking his balance seemed to be tested with every step that he took, until he decided to climb up the slide that was designed for exiting not entering the Wendy house.

After several failed attempts of climbing up and instantly sliding back down again, from my vantage point on the window ledge I held out my hand and placed it under his little right foot. This was the leverage he had been searching for; he was now climbing to the top.

He knew nothing of my helping hand, he was unaware of the part I had played in his success, he was equally unaware of the part he had played in reminding me why I loved the psychology of achievement so much. We all have benefited at some point in our lives form a helping hand, a kind word, a new sense of direction or even just to have confirmed we are on the right track. I know I have benefitted from meeting people who have massively influenced my life and my career.

People whose knowledge ignited within me a passion and enthusiasm to make positive changes in my life, they allowed me to discover just like my little wobbly friend, I didn't have to keep sliding back down and that life was not always going to be up hill. Giving others a helping hand to make positive changes in their lives always gives me the same feeling I had when helping my little wobbly friend.

As for Bella and my wobbly friend I can only hope that they continue to radiate out that beautiful smile, that loving personality and above all to continue to be the best they can be. If I can play any small part in helping them or any other person to be the best they can be in life, then I will have achieved the very essence of life itself.

> *Success is nothing more than a few simple disciplines, practised every day, while failure is simply a few errors in judgement, repeated every day.*
>
> *It is the accumulative weight of our disciplines and our judgements that leads us to either fortune or failure.*
>
> ~ Jim Rohn ~
> America's Foremost Business Philosopher

The Psychology of Leadership Mastery has evolved as a result of studying three main areas:

4. **Psychology:**

    Psychology is defined as the study of mind and behaviour, the perfect combination for any aspiring leader or business owner to understand and fully integrate into their daily lives.

5. **Leadership:**

    Leadership is defined as the transferring of ideas to the minds of others. How well we transfer those ideas will determine the success we achieve in life, career and business.

6. **Mastery:**

    Mastery is defined as being better today than you were yesterday. Mastery in any subject is a journey not a destination, this way we can continue to improve, achieve and master any area of our lives we choose.

When you put all three together you have the most comprehensive leadership mentoring programme offered anywhere in the UK.

THE PSYCHOLOGY OF LEADERSHIP MASTERY

NOTES / REFLECTION PAGE

www.ingramcontent.com/pod-product-compliance
Lightning Source LLC
Chambersburg PA
CBHW072221170526
45158CB00002BA/696